101

Quips and Quotes

that will equip you for an **A**ma**Z**ing life

ADA ADELEKE-KELANI

AuthorHouse™
1663 Liberty Drive
Bloomington, IN 47403
www.authorhouse.com
Phone: 833-262-8899

Because of the dynamic nature of the Internet, any web addresses or links contained in this book may have changed
since publication and may no longer be valid. The views expressed in this work are solely those of the author and do not
necessarily reflect the views of the publisher, and the publisher hereby disclaims any responsibility for them.

Any people depicted in stock imagery provided by Getty Images are models,
and such images are being used for illustrative purposes only.
Certain stock imagery © Getty Images.

This book is printed on acid-free paper.

ISBN: 978-1-6655-4868-7 (sc)
ISBN: 978-1-6655-4867-0 (e)

Library of Congress Control Number: 2022900340

Print information available on the last page.

Published by AuthorHouse 02/22/2022

authorHOUSE®

Contents

Gift Page

To:

_____

Message:

_____

_____

_____

From:

_____

Dedication

This book is dedicated to:

my Amazing God Who blessed me with this gift that I am serving to the world;

my husband who continues to amaze me with his love and support; and

our sons who fill our lives with their zing.

Acknowledgements

We were not created to do life alone. So even though it is only my name on the cover, I got a lot of help from some of the very special people God placed in my life.

In addition to thanking them for tolerating my many bursts of inspiration, I want to thank my dear family for their support which showed up in different ways including letting me stay in my space when I needed to think, write, or edit. They also helped me by being my beta readers, picking out suitable pictures for some quips when I was undecided and helped me finalize the book's subtitle and the book's cover design too.

I also deeply appreciate and thank my friend (of 30 years), Dr Chinyere Almona, for being my alpha reader. Each of us needs the right people on our side so we remain amazing. Chi, thank you for being on my side.

This section will be incomplete if I do not acknowledge you – yes, **YOU**, my readers. Thank you for taking the time to read and apply the quips in this and my other books in your lives. A special acknowledgement also to all who will buy and give this book as a gift. Thank you for being a source of inspiration and a channel of blessing.

Introduction

Congratulations!! You are holding the 4th book in the *101 Quips and Quotes Book Collection* in your hands.

The first three are:

- 101 Quips and Quotes that will charge and change your life
- 101 Quips and Quotes that will strengthen and sweeten your marriage and family relationships
- 101 Quips and Quotes for Tweens, Teens and Twenties to win with

The first three books are organized around different themes. For this book, I decided to use a slightly different layout from the first three because life happens as it chooses and whatever happens in life, can be described with a combination of the letters in the alphabet. So, I decided to write this book in A-Z sections not chapters because our life doesn't always fit nicely into pre-set chapters despite our best intentions.

Each of the four sections has a maximum of twenty-six quips, each using a word starting with a letter between A and Z as the keyword in the quip. Were you doing the math? Yes, I know that $26 \times 4 \neq 101$. As you read, you will figure out how I got to 101 Quips and Quotes – well, I sure hope you do 😊.

Guess what? In addition to enjoying and applying the quips and quotes in this book, you can also use them as bases for discussions and/or games with your family and friends. See the **Quip Quest** (at the end of the book) which can be played when you with your family physically and/or virtually. I guarantee that you will each amuse and amaze yourselves as you play this game.

Stay amazing

Ada

Section One

1. To **A**chieve more, you need to
   Believe that you can,
   Conquer doubts and fear, then
   Do your best and do not give up!

2.   Like an **e**gg, be defined
by who you become after you are broken.
Your brokenness should increase
your value to the world.

3.   **F**ocus helps you see further and
move faster towards your goals.

4.   According to the world, you survive
by getting more than by giving.
According to the Word, you thrive
by **g**iving more than by getting.

5.   Being **h**appy is not a daily choice,
it is a moment-by-moment choice.

6.   Counter your limitations with your **i**magination and
     achieve your aspirations with your actions.

7.   You may lose your **j**ob…just never lose your joy
     because as the Bible says in Nehemiah 8:10b
     "the joy of the Lord is your strength".

8.   **K**nowing and doing are different and have different rewards;
     knowing God's will and not doing it is a burden
     while knowing and doing the God's will brings you a blessing.

9.   **L**iving a life of service to others is a seed for success.

10. A **m**ap shows you where to go. You can only get there by
     moving in the direction of your desired destination.

11. If you don't stay on the straight and **n**arrow path,
     you will stray to the crooked and destructive path.

12. Do not let the **o**pinions of others be obstacles
     to you taking advantage of opportunities.

13. A little **p**rogress a day will help you go a long way.

14. Every **q**uestion has an answer; if you ask the right question to the right person, you will get the right answer.

15. We're each in a **r**ace but not necessarily in the same space or at the same pace. Face your race.

16.   The only way to <u>s</u>tart is to start.
If you feel too stuck to start, reach out for help.

17.   There is <u>t</u>reasure within you and like a diamond,
you discover it when you are under pressure.

18.   Be thankful that irrespective of all you have
gone through, you did not go <u>u</u>nder.

19.   Your true <u>v</u>alue as a diamond is sometimes
not visible to the untrained eye.

20.   The <u>w</u>ay you think determines what makes you tick or sink.

21.   E<u>x</u>traordinary leaders are willing to
lend a hand to help others up.

22.   What you say "<u>Y</u>es" to today will show up in your tomorrow.

23.   <u>Z</u>est is best displayed when you take positive
action (and carry others along with you).

Section Two

24. You can only **a**chieve and become all you have dreamed of if you are alive and well. So, prioritize self-care.

25. You become what you **b**elieve because your behaviour is based on your beliefs.

26. **C**hange is not a choice…changing is.

27. Your **d**estination will always be a distant desire until you make a decision and take steps in the right direction.

28. You do not meet all of others' **e**xpectations of you, so why do you expect people to meet all of your expectations of them?

29. You cannot stay in your cocoon forever otherwise you will never **f**ly. Ask the butterfly.

30. To be **g**reat, be grateful for the people you meet and interact with everyday.

31. **H**istory happened. What you make happen for yourself and others becomes history eventually.

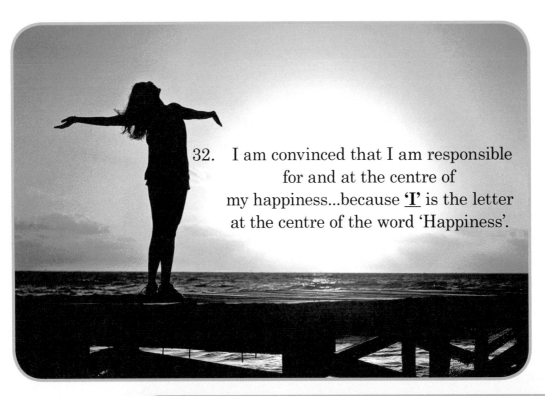

32. I am convinced that I am responsible for and at the centre of my happiness...because '**I**' is the letter at the centre of the word 'Happiness'.

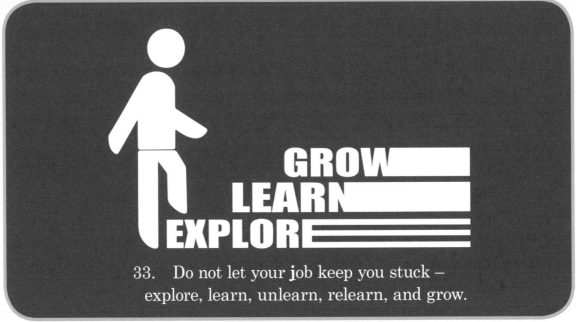

GROW
LEARN
EXPLORE

33. Do not let your **j**ob keep you stuck – explore, learn, unlearn, relearn, and grow.

34. **K**nowledge is only the starting point for wisdom; wisdom shows in your proper application of knowledge.

35. You can live the **l**ife you have always wanted. LIFE is simply Living Intentionally and Fully Everyday while making your way and enjoying your journey through the maze of life.

36.   You can go off track with one **m**isstep.

37.   When you get a '**N**o', use it as an opportunity
to get to learn and know more.

38.   Irrespective of the **o**bstacles you face, achieving the
outcomes you desire starts with your outlook.

39.   Your **p**ast should be your launching pad for
your future not the place of residence.

40.   The **q**uest to arrive at your destination starts with one step.

41.   You cannot demand **r**espect, but you can decline disrespect.

42.   **S**top now and again to evaluate and
ensure that you are still on track.

43.   No one will **t**reat you better than you treat yourself…
be kind to yourself – you are worth it.

44. Sometimes we stop because we are stuck or we get stuck because we stopped – either way, there's no progress. Get **u**nstuck and keep moving.

45. Stay focused on your **v**ision; derision is just a diversion – ignore it.

46. Life happens in **w**aves...you decide whether you will conquer the waves or if they will conquer you.

NO MORE EXCUSES

47. When you e**x**cuse yourself from excuses, you are on the path to exceeding your expectations of yourself.

By Frits Ahlefeldt

48. <u>Y</u>ou are either part of the problem or
part of the solution…you decide.

49. Being in the same time <u>z</u>one with others does not mean
that you are in the same time-of-life zone with them.

Section Three

50. Live an ACE life: ACE (appreciate, compliment and encourage) others now and again.

51. Taking root helps you break through barriers and blossom.

52. In being all things to all men...be a Christian in all things. Don't be a **c**hameleon Christian.

53. **D**iamonds, irrespective of size, shine when properly polished. You will also shine when properly polished.

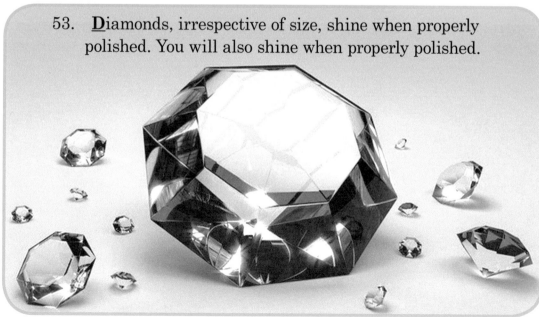

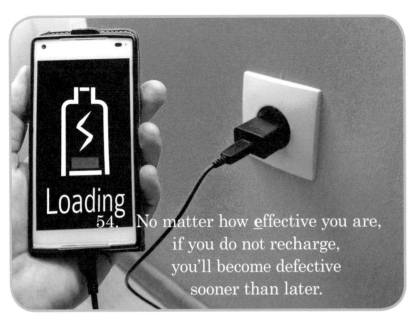

54. No matter how **e**ffective you are, if you do not recharge, you'll become defective sooner than later.

55. **F**altering, falling or failing is not the end of your world...it is just the beginning of a new set of steps. Learn from toddlers...get up and keep going.

56.   Things may not always be **g**reat,
      but we can choose to always be grateful.

57.   To listen with your **h**eart, you need to be silent in your head.

58.   God does not **i**solate Christians from storms, rather
      He insulates and insures us in the storms.

59.   It is better to be **j**oyful even if you are jobless than
      "joy-less" and "job-less". Joy is a source of strength
      and will get you to being joyful and "job-ful."

60.   **K**nowing the ways of God is of no value
      if you are not doing His will.

61.   The **l**ight of God within you makes your life
      light (and free from the burden of sin).

62.   If you do not **m**anage your time others will manage it for you.
      No one can value your time more than you.

63.   Saying "**N**o" to the wrong things could impact
      everything that is right in your life.

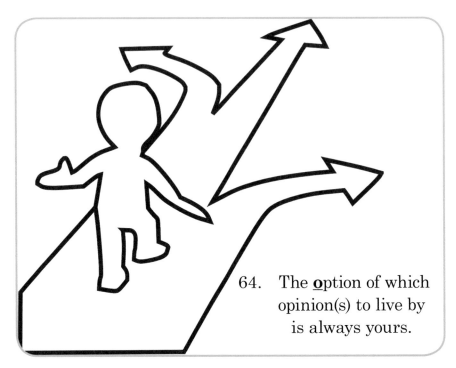

64. The **o**ption of which opinion(s) to live by is always yours.

65. You will only achieve what you desire if you are willing to pay the price for the **p**rize.

66:    The quality of your roots (in God) will determine if you survive, let alone thrive.

67:    If you change your perspective, you will see the rocks in your way as stepping stones.

68.   The right **s**teps set you up for success and
the wrong steps set you up for learning from failure.

69.   **T**rust thrusts relationships to the next level.

70.   It is not wise to condemn what you do not **u**nderstand.
If you do, chances are that you will look foolish
after you take the time to understand.

71.   Your best success is becoming
a better **v**ersion of yourself each day.

72.   **W**ho and what you focus on determines
whether you succeed or not.

73.   A bad e**x**perience yesterday is not a valid excuse for not
extending love today...
who knows, tomorrow you may need love
to be extended to you.

74.   You are **YO**Unique and there's a niche
no one else but you can fill.

75.   **Z**eal is real when you feel it in your bones and
work it out and have action as your seal.

Section Four

76.   Your **a**ttitude, not just your aptitude, determines your altitude.

77.   You don't run out of **b**lessings when God blesses you,
especially when you run out to be a blessing to others.

78.   You will be amazed how much we can each
and all **c**omplete if we stopped competing with each other
and start complementing each other.

79.   Do not let your **d**reams die as dreams.
Do something so they come true.

80.   **E**nrich the world not the grave, die empty.
To die empty, you need to live and give fully daily.

81.   **F**ocus on shining. Stars do not compete with each other...
they just focus on shining. You are a star so do the same.

82.   Everything you go through in life is meant to deepen your roots
and ensure your **g**rowth and fruitfulness.

83. God never has and will never fail because He doesn't know how to. **H**old on to Him, and you'll get to your finish line.

84. **I**nsight from God, equips you with foresight for your life.

85. **J**ealousy blinds and robs you of relationships that can take you to the next level you desire. Watch out and avoid it.

86. **K**ind and candid compliments complement relationships.

87. Whatever kind of **l**ife you want to live, live it kindly.

88. I daresay that **m**oments matter more than milestones. So make your moments more memorable... then your milestones will comprise memorable moments.

89. **N**ourish what you cherish because what you nourish, will flourish and what you do not nourish will perish.

90. Everyday we have an **o**pportunity to do something to make things happen or do nothing and only read what has happened.

91. No one has ever been able to move forward successfully while living in the **p**ast.

92. Don't **q**uit, don't sit, just refit yourself with grit and get back in the game. Move forward bit by bit.

93. Be grateful for the "thorns" that protect you and help your life remain **r**osy.

94. Take **s**teps even if they are baby steps.
Baby steps are STEPS:
Specific Tasks Evidencing Progress Steadily.

95. **T**ime keeps going…not waiting.
You should keep going…and stop waiting,
to get to where you want to.

96. **U**nderstanding the value of changing seasons will help you appreciate the gift and glory of change.

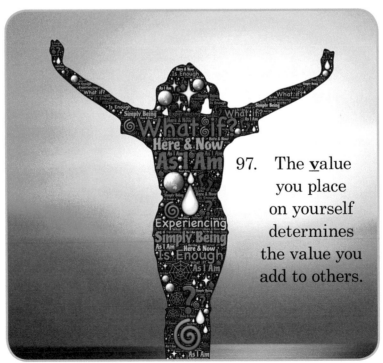

97. The **v**alue you place on yourself determines the value you add to others.

98. <u>W</u>allowing in worry swallows up your strength.

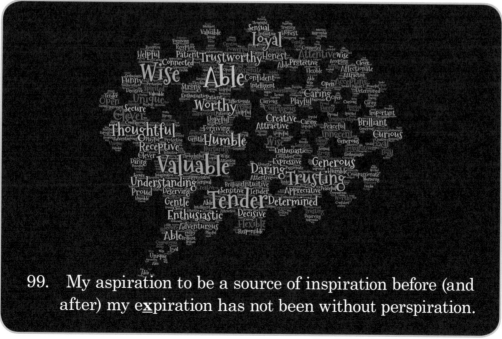

99.   My aspiration to be a source of inspiration before (and after) my e<u>x</u>piration has not been without perspiration.

100.   If you delay long enough, tomorrow will become **y**esterday. So, take action today.

101. The level of your daily **z**ing underpins having an amazing life.

Additional Boosting Comments

1. Learn to accept that the world does not revolve around you.
Even the sun goes dark for the moon and stars to shine.
It is what it is.
– 'Leke Kelani

2. Beauty is subjective.
Do not let others dictate what you find beautiful.
– Oba Adeleke

3. When we commit our ways to the Lord,
He's committed to doing what's best for us.
– Ibunkun Adeleke

Quip Quest

Number of Players: 2 or more

Instructions:

1. Decide on someone to choose 1 quip (you can use a coin to decide if only 2 players or a dice if more than 2 players).
2. Challenge yourselves to rephrase or come up with a similar quip using the same key word within 2 minutes.
3. Set a timer and the person who comes up with the most original quips in the shortest time gets 2 points and gets to choose the next quip to be rephrased.
4. The person with the highest points after 10 minutes wins.

If you email your quips to: <u>QuipCorner@outlook.com</u>, you may have a chance of being featured in the Quip Corner with Ada (YouTube Channel) or in in a future book (after the originality of the Quip is confirmed and your permission is obtained).

Q-Notes

Conclusion

It is already challenging writing a book filled with quips and quotes for everyday life. However, I decided to challenge myself further by using each letter of the alphabet as the keyword in each quip.

And because I believe, more like I know ☺, that we are all innately creative, I created and added the **Quip Quest** as a bonus. It can be played with your family, friends, and in other small or large groups, physically and virtually.

I hope that in addition to having fun with this game, you will find fulfillment as you apply these quips in your life and share them with others.

I trust that you enjoyed reading this book and will refer to it regularly because it is one of those books that you never really finish reading – and this applies to the other books in this collection.

I look forward to hearing from you. You can contact and follow me on:

 Lin.ktree: @QuipQueenAda

For coaching or speaking engagements please email me: PEAAKKonsulting@gmail.com

Readers' Reviews on
101 Quips and Quotes Books

Autographed copies of my books can be ordered at:
https://101quipsandquotes.blogspot.com

101 Quips and Quotes
that will charge and change your life

"Every morning, I start my day with reading something of high value that soothes my soul. I've added Ada's book to my routine. The content of her book is soul soothing. It's like having tea with a wise family member who gives you solid life advice and you feel better for having spent that time with that person. That's Ada's book." ~ Gail

""101 Quips and Quotes" is a well blended, easily readable book with refreshingly rich illustrations from a GOD-fearing woman.
Her passion and love for humanity is unique and infectious.
She takes the reader on a provocative journey with insightful and biblical keys on changing our thought patterns and making wise choices that lead to life, not death in this troubled and turbulent world." ~ Nnennaya O

101 Quips and Quotes
that will strengthen and sweeten
your marriage and family relationships

"101 quips and quotes that will strengthen and sweeten your marriage and family relationships offers you nuggets that you can retain in your heart and even review quickly whenever you need too.
These quips are always relevant because they are truths that transcend generations." ~ Uyi

"Great book for a quick read and reference for all your personal relationships." ~ Viola M

101 Quips and Quotes
for Tweens, Teens and Twenties to win with

"The quips and quotes in the book are not just for tween, teens and twenties. They are life quotes for anyone and everyone. Easy to understand and great conversation points. Thanks Ada! Another excellent book." ~ Geri

Printed in the United States
by Baker & Taylor Publisher Services